# IT Asset Management

A Pocket Survival Guide

# IT Asset Management

## A Pocket Survival Guide

MARTYN HOBBS

IT Governance Publishing

Every possible effort has been made to ensure that the information contained in this book is accurate at the time of going to press, and the publisher and the author cannot accept responsibility for any errors or omissions, however caused. No responsibility for loss or damage occasioned to any person acting, or refraining from action, as a result of the material in this publication can be accepted by the publisher or the author.

Apart from any fair dealing for the purposes of research or private study, or criticism or review, as permitted under the Copyright, Designs and Patents Act 1988, this publication may only be reproduced, stored or transmitted, in any form, or by any means, with the prior permission in writing of the publisher or, in the case of reprographic reproduction, in accordance with the terms of licences issued by the Copyright Licensing Agency. Enquiries concerning reproduction outside those terms should be sent to the publisher at the following address:

IT Governance Publishing
IT Governance Limited
Unit 3, Clive Court
Bartholomew's Walk
Cambridgeshire Business Park
Ely
Cambridgeshire
CB7 4EH
United Kingdom

*www.itgovernance.co.uk*

First published in the United Kingdom in 2011
by IT Governance Publishing.

ISBN 978-1-84928-292-5

## ABOUT THE AUTHOR

Martyn Hobbs has been working in the IT industry for over 20 years. In that time, he has held many roles, including managing large support centres, service desks and service delivery functions. Martyn has also held various consultancy and pre-sales roles, working within a broad cross section of industries. He has been a guest speaker at many industry conferences and events, and also has an excellent reputation as an advisor amongst his peers and within his customer base. At present, Martyn is a senior partner in an IT consultancy business, specialising in Service Management and associated toolsets. He works from his base in Cambridgeshire, where he lives with his wife and three daughters.

# ACKNOWLEDGEMENTS

We would like to thank the reviewers of the manuscript, Jared Carstensen, Manager, Deloitte & Touche and Chris Evans, ICT Compliance Manager, London Fire Brigade, for their helpful comments.

ITIL® is a Registered Trade Mark of the Office of Government Commerce in the United Kingdom and other countries.

# CONTENTS

# INTRODUCTION

A number of years ago, there was a great panic in the world of computing, IT and electronics. The fact that the world was about to enter a new millennium sent 'experts' dashing and chasing in all directions, spreading the word that any electronic device that was in use relied on time and date information and, as such, was unlikely to continue working as soon as the clocks struck midnight on 1st January 2000. For many, this would mean an opportunity to sell their services – some at greatly inflated prices, due to the ever-increasing levels of distress that this pending doom was bringing. It also meant, however, that in organisations throughout the developed world, many long hours would be spent looking long and hard at all the devices that could potentially fail. Many hours of effort were wasted contacting manufacturers, desperately seeking assurance that all the machines we relied upon would not, in a confused silicon stupor, suddenly power down at midnight and drag civilisation to a grinding halt.

With the gift of hindsight, we now know that all of the prophesied doom did, in the end, just not happen. Machines and computers carried on working, the world as we knew it did not stop, and so, on the first working day back – 8 am on Tuesday 4th January – everyone breathed a collective sigh of relief and thanked all those expensive consultants for working so hard on our behalf for months prior to this non-event. Many organisations then spent the rest of the financial year licking their wounds, wondering exactly where all their hard-earned cash had gone and what value they had actually seen from spending it.

But isn't this situation so typical of the IT industry? We spend and invest so much in the 'next big thing', but, as soon as it arrives, it becomes part of the everyday landscape, part of the office wallpaper, something that we just expect to happen day in, day out, and come to rely on. And, of course, we then start to look forward to the 'next next big thing', wondering just how marvellously that will change our lives again, and failing to look back and learn the all-important lessons from our previous expended efforts and achievements.

And so it was with the dawning of the new millennium, with everyone in the IT industry so relieved that the modern world had not collapsed around their ears, shaking the dust of the New Year from their shoes and starting to look forward to the next challenge, that many failed to look back at the debris that the last 6–12 months had created – the potential value that may have lain within the remnants of the chaos and the real opportunity that they could have grasped to get some return on their investments.

Maybe they were so relieved that they preferred not to be reminded of the pain they had gone through. Maybe they were just so embarrassed that they had wasted so much money on experts with little or no hope of any real return. Maybe they had moved on to look for the 'next big thing' too soon. Or maybe it was just that, at that time, the IT world was very male-dominated, consisting of mere blokes who just 'high fived' on their ability to avert a major catastrophe and moved on.

Shame on you, IT managers at that time, for, in your eagerness to move on, you failed to notice that in the debris of the millennium bug there was all the information you would ever have wanted to have known about your systems, devices and computers at that moment in time. There was the make, model, serial number, BIOS level, box colour, power consumption, physical location, business usage, support information, relationships to other systems, etc. In short, there was everything that you would have needed to fully understand your environment and manage your future in a controlled manner.

Shame on you for failing to see the opportunity to take that information, protect it, and place around it process and procedure to make sure that it would continue to be updated and be of value.

And now, because you have picked up this guide, my guess is that you have a desire to gain that level of information once more as you have issues that you need to sort out, issues that – by managing this information effectively from 4th January 2000 – would have been kicked into touch, issues that are causing you pain and keeping you awake some nights. But here we stand, unable to return to that glorious time (unless we employ Dr Who, Captain Jean-Luc Picard, or a similar time-travelling genius to transport us back across the years). Let's just take a moment to reflect on our misfortune – a minute's silence, if you will, sitting quietly to consider the mistakes of our forebears and contemplate the challenge that now lies before us.

But, let us not give up at this early stage. Take confidence from the fact that you are not alone and, as such, that the rewards to be gained from effectively implementing Asset Management are many and worthwhile. I hope that the following chapters of this guide will provide you with some structure for your project, some food for thought that will move you forward towards your goals, and that you will feel revived and energised in your desire to gain control of your environment.

### *Remember:*

- You are not the first, and you definitely will not be the last, to find yourself in this situation.

# CHAPTER 1: OPERATIONAL CHAOS?

## *What are the challenges?*

- How can I get better visibility of my IT environment?
- How do I reduce the number of major outages that keep happening?
- Do I need to reinvent the wheel just for my organisation?

So, as mentioned in the introduction to this guide, I reckon it's a fairly safe bet that if you are reading this book then you feel that you have some issues that you need to sort out with regards to your IT infrastructure and the management of that environment, and possibly that you think those problems are linked to a lack of information, structure or control.

Well, if you feel that just walking into the office on a Monday morning means that you will be greeted by chaos and failure day after day, week after week, then there is a good chance that you need some structure in how your configurations are organised and some order in the working practices and processes that you follow every day.

At the outset of the project, it is important to understand what you want to get out: your objectives. These should relate to your view of what is wrong and needs to be achieved. Set those objectives in concrete, put them to one side, and return to them regularly throughout your project life cycle. Do not be pressured into changing your priorities, the order of your objectives or, in fact, your overall goals (unless they threaten to get you fired, in which case discretion is definitely the better part of valour!).

From my experience, the value of process and procedure is never to be underestimated and in the Information Technology Infrastructure Library (ITIL®) there can be found an excellent template for creating the structures and foundations upon which you can base your infrastructure and environment.

Within the ITIL® framework there are, without doubt, a number of processes that will be key to your success. In ITILv2®, the three main support processes – Incident Management, Problem Management and Change Management – were introduced, and even though the ITIL® framework has undergone rewrites since that time, these key processes are still the ones that the IT support departments in most organisations live and die by, regardless of whether or not they operate as clearly defined or more integrated combined managed processes.

So here is a quick five-minute, common sense, practical introduction to those key processes and their purpose:

**Incident Management**

Incident Management is about recovering the service that the customer was using and relying upon to carry out their everyday work. This service will, for whatever reason, no longer be available, or is no longer responding in the way that the customer expects. The process of Incident Management is all about recording the failure and defining the steps to be taken to restore the service back to an operational state, so that the end-user can continue on with their work. It involves capturing how the end-user presented the issue to the support desk, the time it took and the resources that were used to restore the service, as well as what action was finally taken to restore the service.

Overall, Incident Management is a reactive process – reactive, as it is instigated when the end-user has an issue – and remains open until the service has been restored.

**Problem Management**

Problem Management is about investigating what causes the failures that we record in Incident Management, or, in fact, in any other area within our environment. It involves bringing together resources to investigate the possible root causes of the failures and pulling together enough information to propose potentially permanent resolutions. In this way, future major failures can be averted, or the level of minor failures within the organisation can be reduced.

In summary, Problem Management is a much more proactive and contemplative process, that takes time to consider all the facts and thinks through possible solutions before proposing the best resolution to be implemented via the Change Management process.

## Change Management

Change Management is about implementing changes into your environment in a controlled manner. All stages of the implementation, the testing and, potentially, the recovery, are considered, documented and followed, so as to achieve a predicted outcome. The process has a number of control points – that is, go/no go points. These points are considered by the change manager or appointed change related officials, all with the aim of providing the best, most comprehensive and complete view of any possible changes needing to be made to the infrastructure.

In short, Change Management is the gatekeeper process that ensures that a balanced and controlled view is taken on any infrastructure changes and, if a failure should occur, ensures that the service it has affected can be restored in a controlled manner.

## Configuration Management

But, whilst the world of IT was generally concerning itself with the Big Three support processes, there was one process that was frequently overlooked, frequently glossed over and frequently considered to be too much work without bringing quick, obvious results. This process was Configuration Management. This was the process that controlled how and when data was stored within the Configuration Management Database (CMDB). No one really wanted to take the time to get the data within the CMDB in order, and yet it was this data that was actually key to the success of the Big Three processes.

So why on earth would anyone think that the effort required for a decent set of Configuration Management processes was just not worthwhile?

Perhaps it was because Configuration Management was just not as glamorous as the other, more customer-facing processes?

Perhaps it was that we struggled to understand a process that, to all intents and purposes, was not a single process, but a group of processes?

Perhaps it was that we were more comfortable being forced to start a process than being relied on to run a regular audit-type workflow?

Perhaps it was because what we actually needed to kick-start Configuration Management was good old fashioned Asset Management, but we were too proud to admit it or roll up our sleeves and make a start.

Perhaps it was because there were very few decent applications on the market to help us, and those that were there were either over-priced or under-featured?

At the end of the day, when all is said and done, and when the curtain falls (and any other clichés you want to use), there is actually no getting away from the fact that Configuration Management underpins and connects the main support processes, as well as the Service Delivery processes and, in truth, Asset Management is actually part of the fundamental core of it. Without Asset Management, starting any CMDB project and trying to deliver an effective IT service is much like trying to put a roof on a new house without first building the walls. It's just not structural common sense; it's going to take a lot of shoring up and, ultimately, you are likely to be left standing looking at a pile of useless rubble.

Without Configuration Management underpinned by Asset Management disciplines, you will find that your logged incidents are not connected by common data, such as the location, software, manufacturer and OS platform, and you will be unable to understand volumes and linked trends. You will treat every new incident as a fresh instance, unlinked and unrelated to anything else that has happened, save perhaps the user that logs the incident.

Without linked trends and defined configuration relationships in the CMDB, trying to investigate problems to establish root causes will be like trying to find an ice cube in the middle of the Sahara Desert.

Without having an understanding of configuration, knowing which devices support a particular service, being able to understand the ultimate cause and effect of downtime on the end-user community and being able to identify potential single points of failure – all of which are defined within a CMDB – you will be unable to make an informed decision about major changes in your organisation, and will probably move from one major disastrous change implementation to the next.

### *Remember:*

- Better visibility comes with creating order from chaos, which takes some organising!
- There's no need to reinvent the wheel – ITIL® may hold some or all of your solutions.
- A beautiful house is only built by completing key tasks in the correct order.

## CHAPTER 2: BASIC LOGISTICS AND INVENTORY

### *What are the challenges?*

- How do I set the best scope, range and remit for my project?
- Is this project going to have any impact on my organisation?
- How do I make sure that the project doesn't run out of steam?

So, having been forced to consider how we missed our major opportunity to prevent our current predicament way back at the turn of the century, and also having taken a look at the situation that we may now find ourselves in, how do we consider moving forward and getting our house in order?

Well, first be assured that investment in an Asset Management project will deliver a return. This may not come at first – when the majority of groundwork and discovery is being put in – but as the project starts to mature and the information that is gathered is pieced together, you will start to find opportunities to make savings. Some savings will be larger and some smaller, but all of them will be opportunities nonetheless, creating a snowball effect as your project rolls downhill, gathering more and more mass on its journey, and becoming a bigger and bigger force for positive change within your organisation.

So where to start? As a song writer once put it, 'At the very beginning'. This is, of course, a very good place to start and, in this case, it's with a basic inventory. The primary desire is to know what you own, what these things are in detail, where they are physically, and even, perhaps, who the primary users of them are.

So what do you own? Do you have any physical proof of purchase? Let's make an assumption here: let's say that equipment bought during the last five years could feasibly still have an active role in your organisation. Goodness knows, I've seen some organisations that are surviving on technology well over ten years old, either because they haven't bothered to change it, haven't had the capital to spend on a refresh or, in some instances, have not been able to find any better alternative.

This means that at the outset you should not be too surprised about what you may find in your organisation's dark and dingy corners. It also means that you cannot rely on procurement information alone to complete your inventory – even having five years of comprehensive records may not be going back far enough to take everything into account.

Let's start to consider the various areas that your project may take you into, so that we can start to break the workload down and prioritise. For example, if we think about hardware generally, this could be split into the following:

- Desktop hardware
- Portable computer
- Server hardware
- Communications hardware
- Peripherals and plug-ins
- Telecommunication equipment
- Handheld devices
- Virtual machines.

Trying to capture all of these items in one go would be too much for all but the most small and compact environments. Capturing server hardware and associated communications equipment can be a bit easier, as the majority of this will typically reside in a secure server or computer room and, as such, is unlikely to physically move around greatly while you try to carry out an audit.

Desktop and portable hardware – laptop equipment, for example – will pose a bit more of a challenge. Nothing will be able to beat completing a physical audit, but actually capturing laptop users in the building may be difficult if they are field- or home-based staff. So some other tactics may need to be considered.

One of the ways to capture inventory data would be to engage with your end-user community in some way to ask if they have equipment that they believe is assigned to them or that they take responsibility for. You can assume, in the majority of cases, that an organisation will at least know who is on the payroll and so who is likely to be using a company asset. If that kind of report is unavailable, then there is a good chance your organisation is leaking money like a sieve and will not be around for too long; so it may be time to start looking for a new job!

Sending out an initial e-mail to all those on your employee list (asking for information via voting buttons, for example), will give you a baseline in terms of the number of items that you will need to start looking for and registering. On average, when considering traditional IT usage amongst corporate employees, you can consider that there will be no more than two devices per employee that connect to your IT systems. That's considering traditional devices (i.e. desktops, laptops, or other PC-style workstation devices) but, in this new decade, with the dawning of what's termed as the millennial generation, we find that typically the number of connected devices is somewhat higher – on average closer to four devices per individual, as this will now typically include phones, smart phones, handhelds and tablet devices, to name but a few.

Investigating the possibility of a management application or discovery tool that could be deployed in your environment to find every connected device would be a good move, as such devices yield a high percentage of visibility. You will, however, need to set aside a budget for purchasing such an application.

Looking at reports from your domain name servers also can yield an understanding of the devices within your environment, as they will show both the number of IP addresses that are consumed and provide links to the device names.

Now, although I would recommend you start by building a comprehensive hardware asset listing, I am aware that a major objective in IT Asset Management is usually software licence control. I am a firm believer that software is always installed on something; it may be accessed and used by someone, but it has to reside somewhere and so, if you do not know where all your hardware is, how can you ever, hand on heart, be certain that somewhere in your organisation there isn't a PC with £25,000 worth of un-catalogued software installed, just sitting waiting to introduce you to the legal processes associated with prosecuting under-licensed customers?

Finally, once discovered, you will need to identify each device individually, so as to avoid double-counting. One way to do this is to introduce asset numbers, although this does create specific issues with regards to recognition if the label is removed and linking to the electronic identity that will be seen on your network. The key thing to remember is that you will need a unique identifier for each device – even if it is just the manufacturer's serial number – and that unique identifier needs to be recorded accurately and will be the key that holds all the rest of the asset information together.

### *Remember:*

- 100% records of inventory is a target to aim for, but 100% accuracy of your data is an absolute necessity for data integrity.
- Implementing and maintaining inventory-related processes will be a catalyst for cultural change.
- Without the solid foundation of an inventory, the rest of the house will be unstable.

# CHAPTER 3: KEEPING IT FRESH

## *What are the challenges?*

- How do I find the best place to start?
- How do I keep my customers on my side?
  How do I manage changes, such as additions and removals?

When it comes to interacting with end-users, remember that they often need little excuse to blame the tools that they have been given to carry out their role, and their perception of having
out-of-date or underpowered equipment is sometimes enough alone to increase the volume of calls to your support desk. Whilst there may be situations where using old equipment to carry out a specific task within your infrastructure is appropriate, when it comes to your users, their own perceptions are most definitely their reality.

With this in mind, take a detailed look at your support statistics to see if you can identify any hardware-related trends – it may be machines of a certain make or model or, in fact, a combination of application and machine specifications (for example, all PCs with less than 3GB of RAM running a specific application). Do this across both desktop and laptop areas and make a list of any areas that seem to be affecting call volumes. Then look at your whole environment to understand how many machines may require changing.

Whilst there is some value in performing upgrades and new image builds, keeping active machines within the standard two- to three-year manufacturer warranty periods, if managed efficiently, will be more cost-effective than paying for additional maintenance contracts as insurance against failure.

With an understanding of how many machines you want to replace, go to the market place and get an estimation of the cost. Also consider a programme of change rather than a single big bang approach, setting up a schedule of change which rolls out the new machines gradually. This approach will also help minimise the impact on individual areas of the business.

In discussions with your chosen hardware manufacturer, include the possibility of them creating or duplicating a machine image for your new machines, as well as the possibility of them assigning asset numbers in line with your proposed schema. In this way, when you receive a shipment, you will have most of the software build completed and also a simple update to your asset inventory listing of the new machines.

For a successful ongoing Asset Management process that maintains a high level of accuracy, it is paramount that you identify and control the 'doors' into and out of your organisation that IT assets may travel through. Only by the process of identifying new or additional equipment and highlighting and verifying old, retired or lost equipment, can you make sure that your asset database is maintained accurately.

The procurement process is clearly the most obvious 'door' into your environment, and having your hardware supplier provide you with information that is accurate and relevant will make your records easier to update. Also consider other methods by which equipment may arrive in your environment – either through other procurement channels that you do not control or via individual users that bring in equipment that they wish to use in the company environment. Make sure that you are able to maintain control and that you strive to gain communication with new equipment. Also ensure that the support lines are clearly drawn, so that you can easily identify what you need to support and what you can save effort on.

Similarly, with the exit points from your environment, you have a responsibility to ensure that any equipment that is to leave your organisation is effectively disposed of and that all data that is inappropriate out of the context of your organisation is removed effectively. It is also your responsibility, wherever possible, to identify equipment that has not been officially removed but is termed as missing. Using automated inventory tools and setting date criteria within which reports can be made regularly may go some way to help identifying equipment that 'walks' of its own accord.

### *Remember:*

- Start by looking for changes that will have the most impact or have the most positive effect.
- Without customers, you probably wouldn't have a job, so keep their satisfaction as a top priority.
- Identify the entry and exit points for assets in your environment and put in place processes and controls to manage them effectively.

# CHAPTER 4: LICENSED TO BILL

## *What are the challenges?*

- What do I do if I'm told software licence compliance is a priority?
- The last thing I want is to have to pay a huge bill, but will it be worth the effort?

There's a great quote from the author Rudyard Kipling which starts:

'If you can keep your head when all about you are losing theirs and blaming it on you ...'

The point of the quote is to suggest that keeping yourself calm in a situation where you are surrounded by chaos means that you have a level of maturity beyond that of most people. I much prefer this version from a popular comedian that goes a little like this:

'If you can keep your head when all around you have lost theirs, then you probably haven't understood the seriousness of the situation.'

As was mentioned in a previous chapter, one of the most frequent driving forces behind a programme of Asset Management is the desire to ensure that software licence compliance is achieved or, put simply, to know that you are only using software that you have proof of purchase for and is legal to be used in your organisation.

When it comes to managing a chaotic IT environment, there may perhaps be a little truth in both quotes, as your view of task priorities may be vastly different from another individual's. Whilst it may be that you have all the facts at your fingertips – facts that enable a calm, balanced decision to be made – there is always an outside chance that you perhaps don't fully understand the potential impact that something may have if not resolved quickly.

The same could be said of your understanding of the impact of not being licence compliant, namely that perhaps one of the major software manufacturers has already been knocking on your corporate door and your superiors are trying to work out how best to deal with their approaches.

To manage your software asset inventory effectively, there are a number of key building blocks that you will need in place. If the desire is just to check and balance the number of installed software products against the procurement records you have available, then the building blocks that you require will be:

- A full inventory of all installed programmes for each machine in your environment
- A full list of all software procured, containing all valid or potentially valid products.

$$\frac{\text{Purchased licences} - \text{Installed licences}}{\text{Software licence compliance}}$$

**Figure 1: Compliance equation**

When it comes to producing an accurate inventory of installed software – one that is auditable by a software manufacturer – you will first need that comprehensive hardware inventory that we discussed in previous chapters. Logic dictates that software always has to be installed on a computer – sometimes physically, sometimes virtually, sometimes you may even connect from one computer to another to use the software – but the plain fact is that software has to be installed to be used, and so knowing where all your machines are enables you to complete a full, honest and accurate software inventory.

To create a record of purchased licences, you will need to go back through all of the records that may contain a reference to software purchases. As a guideline, the past five years is probably a reasonable amount of time to consider.

Put together a single list, perhaps in spreadsheet format, and include the software manufacturer, application name, version number, vendor and purchase date.

It may also pay to gather any maintenance contract information in a separate sheet as you are collating the information, as this could be used in the project further down the line.

When creating the list, remember to check for the following sources:

- All paper orders held in records
- All electronic orders held in records, including e-mails and documents
- All hardware procurement records, as the major PC manufacturers can also ship applications with new machines.

With both sets of information now to hand, you will be able to match the number of software applications you have purchased against the number of software applications you know you have installed. That resulting number will either be a positive figure – which tells you you have bought more than you have installed, or a negative number – which means you have installed more than you have bought. Once the list is sorted into software manufacturers, this, put simply, is your software licence compliance summary.

So what now?

Well, if all your numbers are positive, then excellent – you are not only compliant, but have a view of what spare licences you now have. This means that when a customer asks for an additional, or new, application to be added to their workstation you will know if you need to buy any additional software to satisfy their request.

If any of your numbers are negative, this signifies that you will need to take some action. The simplest path to compliance from this point is to purchase software licences to cover your shortfall – which, of course, is the path that most software manufacturers would prefer you to take. But what if your budget is limited, the bill is too large to pay off in one go, or the version of the software needed is no longer for sale?

If you are in the situation where the shortfall or deficit is too large, clearly you will need to establish if the installed software that is under-licensed is actually in use and/or required in the business. Some management tool providers have the ability to establish if an application on a remote machine is used and, if so, how often and for how long. If you have this capability, then set up the monitors and, where possible, start to harvest licences from machines that do not use or no longer have the use for the application. If you are not fortunate enough to have such a tool, a simple customer amnesty may help by surveying the customers with under-licensed software to see if they are able to give up licences that are no longer required.

In most cases, entering a dialogue with the software manufacturer – particularly if they are knocking to ask for compliancy reports – will be of help. A decent software manufacturer will want to know you are concerned that you are under-licensed, will be keen to see your plans to rectify the situation, will want to work with you to ensure that you reach compliance, and will be more likely to grant time to sort out the situation.

If the software licence you require is no longer available in the market place, then again entering a discussion with the software manufacturer should reveal if it is possible to purchase a new licence and still use the old version. Alternatively, you might need to consider an upgrade to the next available licensable version to ensure full compliancy.

### *Remember:*

- Don't try to do things in the wrong order; you will need your comprehensive hardware inventory to lock down your software inventory.
- It usually pays to open a dialogue with your software manufacturer if you are being put under timescale pressures.
- Doing nothing is not an option – it could end up costing you financially and legally.

# CHAPTER 5: PLANNING AERIAL ASSAULTS

*What are the challenges?*

- Understanding the strategic direction of your organisation and how your project will benefit it
- Finding a project sponsor at an appropriate level in your organisation
- Keeping your project sponsor informed and on board.

As with any project that involves making changes to a process in relation to a best practice standard, one of the greatest risks could be seen as a lack of senior management buy-in. Put in simple terms: even if you have the greatest will and perseverance in the world and the determination to see your Asset Management project through to the end, it may still all come to nothing. On the first occasion that someone challenges one of your decisions and escalates the matter to your superior – who then does not back you and overrules your decision – you may as well give up there and then.

If, however, you take the time to do the groundwork with the senior management team, the chances are that the query will go your way and in future it is more likely that your authority will be observed and followed.

So what is the groundwork and what do you need to do to get you to the strongest position possible?

Firstly, you must understand the structure of the upper echelons of your organisation – who reports to whom? In your line management, ultimately where does the buck stop? Now it may be at a senior management level, it could even be at a board level and, in some cases, it may even need to be at the CEO; each organisation will be different.

You are looking to identify a management resource that will act as your project's sponsor – someone that you can get alongside to understand the strategic direction of the company in a clearer way, and someone that will help push your project advantages and benefits at the most advantageous level in your organisation.

Having identified your potential sponsor, try to get alongside this resource to start to understand what makes them tick, what their priorities are and what objectives they may be working to. Plan to continue meeting with your manager – either formally or informally – so that you understand fully and your manager can see that you do, too.

Whenever you get together, ask open and intelligent questions. Certainly, on the first few occasions that you meet it would be good to listen more than you speak – that way, you can start to understand what your manager's goals, aims, concerns and desires are.

Once you feel you have enough insight, think through your project. List how your project will help underpin or advance your manager's goals and prepare to articulate this at your next meeting. In this meeting, it is vital you express the benefits your manager will see from the successful completion of your project. Following this, it is also important you ask for your manager to take up the position of project sponsor – someone you can keep updated and informed about how you are doing and someone that can take your project to the highest level, should you need authorisation for any project-related activity.

Then wait for the response. If it is positive, then accept your manager's support and go and get on with your project. If, for any reason, the answer is negative, listen to the concerns and plan to come back again to address them in full.

Finally, with your project sponsor on board, keep them informed with regular updates on your project's progress. In your communications, make your progress updates clear and concise, ensure your project objectives echo or mirror your manager's objectives and goals and, if asked any questions, make sure that you answer quickly and clearly, so that your project sponsor's confidence in you remains intact.

If there are any issues with project deliverables, escalate quickly and clearly – especially if you believe that any customer in the business is likely to escalate or complain – then make sure that you get to your project sponsor first, so that they are fully informed and aware.

### *Remember:*

- Identify your strongest sponsor in the business and plan to get them on board.
- Try to align your project goals with your project sponsor's goals and corporate strategic goals.
- Keep your project sponsor updated with regular, clear and concise project progress reports.

# CHAPTER 6: DEALING WITH THE LOCALS

*What are the challenges?*

- Enforcing control without losing your customers' good will
- Defining standards that work for your customers
- Maintaining control against customer resistance.

Who was it that once said, 'The customer is always right!'? I'm not sure if anyone would be brave enough to own up to being the first to make that statement, but I reckon they never had to deal with your customers, right?

I much prefer the idea that the customer may think that they are always right but, in truth, they are sometimes misguided, often ill-informed and, I'm fairly sure, regularly doing things just to mess up your day!

However, let us not forget that without them we in IT support would probably not have jobs, so expressing these kinds of views openly is probably not the most politically sound move you will make in your career.

The issue still remains, however, that sometimes customers can be awkward to deal with, particularly when it comes down to subjects such as control, standardisation, and reducing their perception of choice. Those of you that are parents will understand that when your sickly offspring creates and plays up over having to take their medicine because they think it tastes truly awful, we all know that, in fact, this moment of discomfort will be good for them in the long run and their experiencing this bitter taste for a matter of minutes will mean that they will soon return to full health.

The same is true for our customer base. When going through the discomfort of an Asset Management project, there is a good chance that you will have to put in place some fairly strong and robust rules to get you to where you need to be. To some of your customers, these will be akin to cutting off one of their hands, or perhaps oppressing their human rights. However, in reality, if positioned correctly, the customer may see that they have as much to gain from the changes as your department does.

The first thing to do to gain control is to identify all the routes into and out of your environment – this is simple logic. For you to be able to control and keep updated a list of everything that you own and manage, you need to know if anything is added to that list or taken away. It may be a bit of a strange analogy, but think of your environment as a valet parking area. You need to know exactly which customers' cars are parked there and so are your responsibility to look after. When you collect a new vehicle, you book it in and add it to the list, and when you deliver one back, you take it off the list and know that the car is now the customer's responsibility. If you were doing that job, would you ever consider letting the customers park or collect their own car? Would you consider removing the security in-and-out barrier, or the cameras that record the number plates of every vehicle going in and out? Of course, you wouldn't, as fairly quickly you would lose track of what was your responsibility and who knows what might happen?

A similar approach must be taken to controlling assets within an IT environment: you must control the entry points and exit points, so that you can keep your asset register up to date. But, unfortunately, this is not as simple as sticking cameras and barriers on the doors to your office and then enforcing a stop and search policy with your customers. It is true that the doors, windows, tunnels and escape hatches into and out of your environment will be used, either deliberately or inadvertently, by your customers. It may well be, for example, that they deem it to be much quicker and easier than popping to the local computer store to get a copy of the software they need and then claiming it back on expenses. Or, perhaps, just bringing in that new tablet device to plug into the corporate network suits their diary management habits better than trying to justify such a business tool to be purchased.

Labelled as a millennial workforce, the new workers that are in our organisations are IT-savvy people – people who have grown up in the PC age and think nothing of having a smart phone that acts as a camera, web browser, GPS system and provider of mobile e-mail and video web conferencing. On top of this, they are able to obtain these devices relatively cheaply via major service providers, who then configure and get them working with relative ease. It is no wonder then that this new millennial workforce can sometimes be at odds with IT departments and their need for control, as it just does not make sense for them to be restricted in any way. As an estimate, the average person now has anything up to four devices for connectivity to the web – be it a phone, smart phone, handheld, tablet, netbook, laptop or traditional desktop device. Addressing the control of this issue whilst maintaining good customer relations can be a minefield. It is also worth considering the fact that this issue is not just asset-related; as more mobile devices are used with ever-growing data storage capacities, the risk of corporate data loss also increases.

So how do you close the doors and ensure that control is in place?

**Define your IT support policy:** Using your comprehensive asset list, confirm the software and hardware that is within your organisation and identify any item that you feel is outside the scope of your support services. A typical rule of thumb would be that if the item is creating issues within your support organisation without adding any business value, then it should potentially be highlighted as an issue. If the item is not in any way business-related, then it should also be highlighted as an issue

**Implement a rigorous procurement policy:** Ensure that it is clearly communicated that only equipment procured by your company and for use within your company should be in operation. Also, introduce a sign-off for all hardware- and software-related orders to ensure that no equipment is ordered via any route other than via the IT and procurement departments.

**Put in place controls for employee expense claims:** Communicate with all management team members that are responsible for expense authorisation, informing them that under no circumstances is any IT hardware or software allowed to be purchased via the expense system. Also, make available a communication channel, so that any questionable items can be verified with you prior to signing off an employee's claim.

**Publish a catalogue of supported devices:** Using your contacts within your organisation, draw up a list of supported activities that are required for the business to operate – for example, remote e-mail access, remote handheld data usage and mobile web browsing devices – then create a list of supported devices that can be used to carry out these functions.

**Redefine support boundaries:** Create a document to communicate with all customers in your organisation, and in that document include the following points:

- Explain the need for control and your desire to increase the levels of service by simplifying and standardising the IT environment.
- Reinforce the rules on procurement, and explain that this is to keep the environment in line with defined standards.
- Publicise the list of supported devices that will be made available to carry out core business tasks.
- Communicate a timescale window, after which support will end on unsupported devices. Explain that during the window, support will be on a 'best endeavours' basis.

With these steps completed, you should be in a better position to control the doors to your environment and, combined with your detailed inventory, your visibility of any changes in the inventory will enable you to deal with any breaches of protocol.

Finally, consider how you are going to capture any equipment that is no longer required. An unused hardware amnesty could help to get the ball rolling – just ask all staff to inform your service desk about any equipment that is no longer used or appears to no longer be in use. Following this, communicate your desire with the management team to ensure that any equipment leaving your organisation does so in a controlled manner, stating the advantages of this approach as follows:

- Potential for re-use of the equipment versus a fresh purchase
- Financial disposal from the asset register
- Removal of all company data before disposal
- Retrieval of any unused software licences
- Identification of any equipment that disappears without authorisation.

### *Remember:*

- Keep in mind that your decision-making needs to appear to be logical.
- Constantly underpin the changes with your desire to improve customer service levels.
- Be prepared to dig your heels in to maintain control.

# CHAPTER 7: AVOIDING EXPENSIVE MISTAKES

*What are the challenges?*

- Making decisions based on someone else's timescales, priorities or demands
- Making sure you have the best tools to do the job
- Making sure you have resources to complete the project.

There is a great notice that I have seen many a time on employees' desks. It usually says something like:

'Please remember that a lack of planning on your part does not automatically constitute an emergency on mine!'

Whilst this statement is usually meant as a light hearted, 'Don't bother me, I'm too busy' message, there is an underlying truth in the statement – one that you will be aware of if you have ever been approached by a colleague who needs a bill to be paid and communicates a threat that, if it is not paid, something bad will happen.

I am reasonably sure that there are some unscrupulous operators in the business world who would, for example, present a software or service renewal notice just days before it is due, giving you little time to react, most situations can be negotiated and so rarely require an instant response. Paying a large bill just because you do not have all the facts to assess the needs and negotiate effectively could, obviously, cost you dearly. This same situation could apply to any one of the following scenarios:

- Paying for a software licence that you do not have installed and you are not using
- Paying for software maintenance, an upgrade, or support for a licence that you are not using

- Paying for hardware to be repaired when it is still covered by a warranty contract
- Buying additional hardware when there is sufficient hardware that can be re-used in your storeroom
- Buying additional server hardware when your existing server farm is underutilised.

All of these situations may make relatively small savings individually – say only £10–20k each per year – but when you add them together it starts to become £50–100k a year, which is no longer small change. This kind of money could potentially be an additional member of your team, if you think about it. As my dear departed grandmother would say, 'Look after the pennies and the pounds will take care of themselves!'

When thinking about Service Management toolsets – and I am talking about the kind of application that manages information about your desktop environment and related infrastructure – there is a cyclical process I refer to as 'the cycle of replacement'. This is a phenomenon that hits the majority of companies that invest in, or rely on, Service Management applications. The cycle works in this way:

An issue is identified: there is something that is affecting the business and needs to be brought under control, so discussions take place at a senior management level to try to define requirements and choose a toolset that will resolve the issue.

A project is put in place to define the requirements and start the selection process. This takes resources from their everyday operations and takes some time. Reviewing the available applications in the market place also involves a fair amount of effort. Eventually, a toolset is chosen, a budget attributed, and the application is purchased and installed into the environment.

Staff are trained and assigned to manage the toolset and work continues, the issue that was first identified having been resolved.

As time goes by, the toolset becomes part of the daily support fabric and is no longer seen as the main priority. The staff that were assigned to work within and manage the toolset perhaps get assigned to other projects, start working in other areas, or maybe even leave the organisation. During these changes and moves, best efforts are made to hand over the toolset management from one resource to another but, at each step, the level of knowledge and expertise is diminished.

Eventually, the Service Management toolset slips into a semi- or un-managed state and, as that happens, an issue is raised that potentially affects the way that the business runs. Someone raises the issue with the senior management and the response is, 'Didn't we buy toolset X to sort that out?', to which the technician replies, 'Yes, but it doesn't work', 'It's completely useless', or perhaps even, 'Do we have that toolset?'

At this point, the cycle starts again and all the investment that was made in the toolset, its selection, implementation, training and management is wasted and written off.

Allowing this cycle to take place alone can waste perhaps £300k of revenue over a three-year period time and time again, if not identified and curtailed. It is not just the cost of the toolset that needs to be taken into account, but also the cost of the resources that are used every time the selection process is undertaken.

If you have a toolset, check to see if it is the latest version – as an upgrade may give you the functionality you require – or fix outstanding issues that are preventing the toolset being used. Verify the capability and functionality you should be having because, although the functionality to resolve your need may be within the toolset, it may just not yet have been configured. Do some research to see what knowledge, experience and training your staff that are supposed to be managing the toolset have had, as, sometimes, fixing the people's knowledge is a quicker route to success.

Finally, try to avoid the primary instinct and temptation to buy new, shiny objects or to recruit new people to fix issues. Be prepared to carry out an investigation to see what resources you have available, what resources are unused in your organisation, or what resources are underutilised. Also, don't just include physical, inanimate resources in your investigation; remember that your most valuable resource – people – should also be assessed to see if they have any spare capacity!

### *Remember:*

- Pay attention to detail and manage your costs at the lowest level and you will gain a greater understanding at a high level.
- Never assume that the only way to fix an issue is to buy a bigger hammer – you may already have the right tool in your tool chest, it is just that you have never been shown how to use it effectively.
- Don't forget about your most valuable resource – your people!

# CHAPTER 8: STICKING TO THE PLAN

In closing, there are a number of phrases that I would like to leave with you that illustrate how important it is that, having started your project, you see it through to the end.

## 'Even the longest journey starts with the first step.'

It is important that, once you have identified the need to run an IT Asset Management project – either by identifying an issue that needs to be resolved or savings that could be made – you go ahead and start an IT Asset Management project. But, in starting your project, do not underestimate the number of times it may take you to complete your objectives.

## 'When up to your neck in alligators, it is easy to forget that your main objective was to drain the swamp.'

Make sure that at the outset of your project you clearly define your goals and objectives, as these will become the core deliverables of your project. On your journey through your project, you may find other advantages, or uncover reasons for the project's successful completion; however, it is important that you keep in mind and keep working towards the delivery of those core objectives.

## 'Keep the main thing the main thing!'

Finally, whatever other challenges are laid at your feet, as you go about your daily grind remember your responsibilities to your customers: your goal to improve their support, your buy-in from management, and the responsibility on your shoulders; who knows, this just may be character building.

# ITG RESOURCES

IT Governance Ltd. sources, creates and delivers products and services to meet the real-world, evolving IT governance needs of today's organisations, directors, managers and practitioners.

The ITG website (*www.itgovernance.co.uk*) is the international one-stop-shop for corporate and IT governance information, advice, guidance, books, tools, training and consultancy.

*www.itgovernance.co.uk/ITIL.aspx* is the information page on our website for ITIL resources.

## Other Websites

Books and tools published by IT Governance Publishing (ITGP) are available from all business booksellers and are also immediately available from the following websites:

*www.itgovernance.co.uk/catalog/355* provides information and online purchasing facilities for every currently available book published by ITGP.

*www.itgovernance.eu* is our euro-denominated website which ships from Benelux and has a growing range of books in European languages other than English.

*www.itgovernanceusa.com* is a US$-based website that delivers the full range of IT Governance products to North America, and ships from within the continental US.

*www.itgovernanceasia.com* provides a selected range of ITGP products specifically for customers in South Asia.

*www.27001.com* is the IT Governance Ltd. website that deals specifically with information security management, and ships from within the continental US.

## Pocket Guides

For full details of the entire range of pocket guides, simply follow the links at *www.itgovernance.co.uk/publishing.aspx*.

**Toolkits**

ITG's unique range of toolkits includes the IT Governance Framework Toolkit, which contains all the tools and guidance that you will need in order to develop and implement an appropriate IT governance framework for your organisation. Full details can be found at *www.itgovernance.co.uk/ products/519*.

For a free paper on how to use the proprietary Calder-Moir IT Governance Framework, and for a free trial version of the toolkit, see *www.itgovernance.co.uk/calder_moir.aspx*.

There is also a wide range of toolkits to simplify implementation of management systems, such as an ISO/IEC 27001 ISMS or a BS25999 BCMS, and these can all be viewed and purchased online at: *www.itgovernance.co.uk/catalog/1*.

**Best Practice Reports**

ITG's range of Best Practice Reports is now at *www.itgovernance.co.uk/best-practice-reports.aspx*. These offer you essential, pertinent, expertly researched information on a number of key issues including Web 2.0 and Green IT.

**Training and Consultancy**

IT Governance also offers training and consultancy services across the entire spectrum of disciplines in the information governance arena. Details of training courses can be accessed at *www.itgovernance.co.uk/training.aspx* and descriptions of our consultancy services can be found at *www.itgovernance.co.uk/consulting.aspx*.
Why not contact us to see how we could help you and your organisation?

**Newsletter**

IT governance is one of the hottest topics in business today, not least because it is also the fastest moving, so what better way to keep up than by subscribing to ITG's free monthly newsletter *Sentinel*? It provides monthly updates and resources across the whole spectrum of IT governance subject matter, including risk management, information security, ITIL and IT service management, project governance, compliance and so much more. Subscribe for your free copy at: *www.itgovernance.co.uk/newsletter.aspx*.

EU for product safety is Stephen Evans, The Mill Enterprise Hub, Stagreenan, Drogheda, Co. Louth, A92 CD3D, Ireland. (servicecentre@itgovernance.eu)